THE SAFE PILOT'S HANDBOOK

Quick airmanship tips to fly safely, from PPL to ATP

Enderson Rafael

FOREWORD

I met Enderson at the time when we were both flight attendants and aspiring pilots, devouring materials related to the art of flying. After several years and many hours of flight, it's time for my friend
(and brother in wings) Enderson to be the one nurturing the winged dreams of his readers.

This guide provides simple, accessible, and assertive information of
great value to aviation enthusiasts, beginners, and professionals alike.
In Brazil we have a saying: "sometimes hangar chat is worth a lesson". That is the feeling I had when I finished reading this book.
Sharing experiences and knowledge is one of the most generous gestures that a human being can have and I truly appreciate the effort

that my friend made gathering precious learning from others and himself.

Whether you are a sport pilot, flight instructor, agricultural pilot, executive pilot, or airline pilot; I'm sure the information on these pages will be helpful and worthy of the time you invested on reading it.

Albert Einstein said once: "If you can't explain it simply, you don't understand it well enough".
So, if you are worried about complicated words and boring explanations, you will be greatly surprised to find out how Enderson is able to approach a subject with sense of humor, simplicity, and expertise. All without losing focus.

Flying is the type of activity that develops like a road, in which decision making and risk management fundamentally pave the way. Every mile behind is like a brick, irreversibly placed. Your wisdom and experience will guide you on how to put the bricks you have on a beautiful but also smooth path.

Whether in the delightful solitude of a solo flight or in the exciting journey of carrying passengers, one thing is certain: those who have knowledge will never be alone. Through our mentors, instructors or, in this case, by reading an excellent book, we are inspired to exercise good practices and act with discipline.

From the time of Icarus to the present day, our greatest challenge is not to overcome gravity; but rather to do it with discipline, zeal for life and for the flying machine.

Those pages will take you to a delightful journey. Welcome aboard and enjoy your reading!

Juliana Torchetti Coppick

- 1 -
RISK ASSESSMENT
The essential mindset

More than anything else, flying is about risk assessment: the safest airplane in the planet is resting in the hangar - if possible, without fuel or battery. Every time we choose to take off, we are assuming a risk. If the level of that risk is acceptable or not, it is, by essence, a gray area. Therefore, in order to work with this kind of issue, the industry created complex risk matrixes, but the idea of this book is far from getting to the intricate matters of management levels of an airline. It is exactly the opposite: we want to make the concepts available to any pilot who is facing the ever-changing environment of the flight, in a simple and comprehensive way.

So, to make it easy, there are two levels of probability and two levels of damage we want you to understand.

Something can be probable or remote. And this thing, if happens, may bring a small damage or a big one. Those are the four variants you, as a pilot, have to play with. If something is likely but the consequences are mild, no need to worry much. If something is possibly fatal but remote, no need to worry much about it either. Now, as things get closer to probable and of serious consequences, that is when you certainly have to do something about them. Of course, severe failures and events usually have very well designed procedures to be dealt with, and if not only on a checklist, some of them are even things a pilot have to memorize - and are much more standardized across the industry than someone would notice at first sight. Nevertheless, each kind of operation is going to have its own needs and challenges, and the idea of this book is to show the reader some of the scenarios that low time pilots could face. But since there is room for it and our objective is not limited to any level of experience - after all, we keep learning throughout our entire careers - we are going to address meaningful situations that also airline pilots may encounter. We intend it to serve both as reminder to experienced pilots, and a stimulus to whoever is aiming to get there. We hope you enjoy the trip, as much as we are happy to share this operational philosophy with you.

-2 -
UNDERSTAND THE REGS
Legal but not clever

One of the easiest ways to maintain your operation on the safe side is keeping it legal. Since many of the rules have been indeed written in blood, much of the regulations are direct learnings from something that didn't use to be covered before and ended up badly. Think of the FAR 91.119, for example. It dictates about minimum safe altitudes, and pretty much none of the low passes you ever saw - except those on the environment of a proper airshow – were legal. Why is that? Because in the beginning there were no rules at all. People were doing whatever they felt like, and many of them found out too late that they have exceeded either their skills, the aircraft capability, or their luck. So, along the years, the regulations, air traffic control, and even the fly by wire came in the way to prevent pilots of doing things they shouldn't. Obviously, an over regulation would make flight maybe even not viable, and in some aspects they still offer a generous amount of free will to pilots and operators. That is when the common sense comes into play, and no need to say, your common sense may be naturally different from mine.

Nevertheless, that is the beauty of life, and this book offers no granted right answer. Instead, you are going to find ways of staying legal, and more than just that, safe.

The first obvious tip – not so obvious to some: drink from the fountain. Regulations are official publications, and they must be known. The basics, for sure. The more detailed ones, you need to have an idea, and mainly, to know where to find them when needed. If flying international, the Jeppesen Textbook and charts are an amazing tool, and in your country, your Civil Aviation Authority publications. They are not on an internet forum, they are not on a friend's memory: they are in the FARs, and it is from there they should be read and understood. Not written by pilots, but lawyers and bureaucrats. Liability is a big deal nowadays, even for general aviation pilots out of the airline environment, and you really need to know where you are getting into, from day one. And since there's still legal margins, let's talk about them.

This chapter title is one of my favorite expressions. It is perfectly possible to be legal but in jeopardy at the same time. And to get you out of any shenanigans, there is a particularly useful concept called "personal minimums". Exactly: forget about the legal minimums, they might be too much for your level of experience, proficiency or even equipment. This applies to let's say, an IFR approach, as much to a performance calculation. Try to not expect too much from yourself or your airplane. "There are no shortcuts for experience", you probably know who said that. Yet, there is no way of getting experienced without being unexperienced before. So, don't be too hard on yourself, you will eventually get there. The most beautiful thing in our job is to retire old – or at least, when you decide it's time to, not when fate says it is. Therefore, don't be jealous of whoever seems to have more skills or hours than you do, just keep learning from them as much as you can. And do not show off: this is a big killer in our business and nobody will give you an honest applause: instead your audience is very likely envious – and you know, envy people don't usually wish the best to their subject.

The Safe Pilot's Handbook – Enderson Rafael

- 3 -
RESPECT THE WEATHER
"Weather" or not going

Antoine de Saint-Exupéry, one of the great aviators – and authors – of all times, used to call it "the peasant truth". When he flew, in the early decades of mail service flight – same time of Elrey Borge Jeppesen, we mentioned before – that truth was even more evident. Flying on open cockpits, with nearly no ground based electronic aids, and of course, no satellite images of the weather ahead, it was obvious for those aviators that they were nothing like the climatized office guy that already accounted for many of the urban workers. Today, we fly on pressurized and climatized offices, and spend most of the time in front of a computer, and if you are an Airbus pilot, you even have a table to grab on. Yet, the machines we fly are exposed to the very Exupéry's "peasant truth", and a great share of our decision-making process has to do with it.

First, you must understand the weather: its past, its present, its future. With that information available, then again you must apply the regs we talked about in the previous chapter. Are you legal to fly with that ceiling and visibility? Is your airplane equipped accordingly? Can you shoot an ILS CAT IIIB approach into today's fog? Then, we get to the personal minimums we also talked about. Am I proficient on IMC flight? Have I ever flown in anything less than 10 miles visibility? And then, the future.

Identifying trends on the weather is something hard to teach, and to be honest, is always a gamble. But of course, you can do some precision educated guess, with narrow margins, and give yourself some room. A pilot must like studying everything related to his or her job, and when it comes to weather it is an endless learning process. You know that thing of walking on a maze where all the walls continually change? That applies for both private pilots sneaking around low-level cumulus or, an airline crew finding its way across the ITCZ over the ocean at night relying on a modern weather radar. Just like the regulations thing, remember of researching on the official channels for radar coverage, forecasts, METAR, ATIS, satellite images and weather charts. Keep it legal, give some margin for yourself, and you will be fine.

4 -
KNOW YOUR MACHINE
"Come, Josephine, in my flying machine"

Before inviting your date – remember of politely asking his or her weight when you do so – to fly with you, is essential that you know your flying machine well. In the airlines, we fly types, that require months of training just to get the right to start flying them, and the learning process of these complex machines is never ending. In general aviation, in the other hand, you are usually going to fly a class airplane, so whatever training you had on it is far from being that specific. It does not mean, though, that they are not complex enough to deserve a comprehensive self-briefing on their characteristics, performance specifications, weight and balance limitations and fuel capacity, consumption, and important speeds and emergency procedures. Remember the "keep it legal" principle? Take a look at the Aircraft Flight Manual or POH – Pilot Operating Handbook, one of them is supposed to be in the aircraft. The weight and balance manifest also should be there. They are all fundamental tools for you to work with, and we hope this is not the first time you think of reading them and applying whatever need to be applied on your operation.

But what about going an extra mile? Getting an extra lesson with a Certified Flight Instructor? Practicing some landings beyond the legal requirements – which are very generous? These are easy things to do, and if you are beginning to get worried about cost, well, in aviation there's little room for cutting safety related costs. But, what can you do for free?

There is a bunch of things, but we will suggest two: younger pilots often come from the home flight simulation background. Use it! It is an amazing tool for instrument flight training and proficiency, as we all know, but also for aircraft familiarization – and trust me, no matter how complex they are. It is an interactive virtual mockup and with some "chair flight", will prove itself a valuable asset. The other suggestion is at the palm of your hand: search on the internet for accidents and malfunctions the model of airplane you are going to fly has been object. It will improve your overall situational awareness and put you a step ahead in the game.

We are all very proud of the airplanes we fly, and although we may have our preferred ones, usually every aviator falls in love with the machine he or she is flying at the moment: the more we know it, the more we like it. From the weird first hours to that day you literally become part of the aircraft it may take some time, and when that happens, is time to think twice: over confidence leads to complacency. So, be comfortable with the plane you fly, but never lose the respect for it or its limits – or your own limits, for that matter. Get to know your model's strengths and weaknesses. And remember: every single plane was designed for a specific mission. Be sure to keep it that way. Smart engineers have saved many pilots from themselves uncountable times, but their gentle hand is distant. Try to not rely on it too much.

- 5 -
HOME BASE OPS
"Take me back to DeLand"

If that sentence does not ring a bell to you, you probably did not get your licenses where I did. But no matter where your base is at, and how far you fly out of it, knowing some stuff about your ground will keep you safe in the air. Charts, the basic. Nevertheless, the diagrams and the green book are just the minimum you need to do. Just like the weather, airports are living creatures, and to anticipate what mood they are into, you need to read the NOTAMs. Destination, alternates, enroute alternates – the most likely you would use, at least – and yes, your base NOTAMs too. Remember, complacency kills, often. Take a glance at them, it will cost you seconds. Believe me: if something is different, you will notice and it will call your attention. But do not skip them altogether. Treat flying back home like any other flight.

And if the sight of your home base on the returning flight is a relief – or at least, as pleasant as it is for most of us – few challenges are more exciting than flying to somewhere you never flew to before, right? So, while home, do your homework. Study the terrain, prevailing weather, check the last day's reports. Again, use the internet: check the satellite images of the ramp and runways, it will enhance your understanding of the airport diagrams in a great amount. Look for some approach videos of your destination, talk to someone who has been there before. Some places even need special requirements like online courses or simulator training, so be aware of those. Listen to its ATC online, if available. And, if you can, why not fly there in advance on your home flight simulation software? Of course, not every destination requires so much preparation, but doing this will certainly make your workload easier when you get there. Visiting a new destination goes well beyond where to drink and eat once you arrive. It requires a dedicated effort to learn your way, both in the skies and on the ground, before you even see it. Briefings are naturally an important piece of that kind of operation. Keep your flying partner in the loop, if you have one. And if you don't, be kind to yourself, make notes, go through the charts before shooting the approach. And remember, the flight is only over when you get your engine OFF and your chocks ON. Do not relax too early, many accidents and incidents happen on the ground of a never visited aerodrome – as they do happen, for similar reasons, in very familiar airports as well.

- 6 -
FLYING FAR AWAY
The farther you go, the more you need to know

The essence of flying is connecting places. So, most of the flying activities are far from being local, instead of crossing from small patches of terrain within a city to actually shrinking the world at nearly the speed of sound while overflying continents and oceans non-stop. But what are the aspects one should have in mind when doing cross countries? Some are pretty obvious, like the range or endurance of your airplane, how to keep it legal through flight plans and local regulations. But some stuff can be out of your radar if you decide in a rush. Let's say you want to fly to another city which is 2 hours away. If your airplane can carry fuel for 5 hours of flight and you have got it topped off, no need for complicated mathematics. You can always save some brain work by being generous on your assumptions. On the other hand, if you are going to be closer to your endurance, then truly careful analysis of your consumption and your alternates must be done to ensure safety. Do you have a strong headwind in route? Any weather deviation? How is the weather at your destination, what is the trend for when you get there? Any runway closures in the NOTAMS? Like we said before, regulations are there to protect pilots from themselves, and that is why you are going to find different minimum endurance requirements for VFR and IFR flights. Nevertheless, those are all minimums. You can always be more conservative, and with time, your estimates will get more accurate.

Just like deep water is safer for a boat, flat and low terrain is safer for an aircraft. Keep that in mind. If your route crosses high terrain, be aware that those either are not friendly ground when it comes to land or overfly. First, because you might not be able to find a place to land at all if you need. If you are flying a pressurized aircraft, you might not be able to descend to a safe altitude if you lose cabin pressure. And some aircraft cannot simply fly high enough to clear some mountain ranges with all or not all their engines working, and even if they do, their performance is going to be extremely limited. Once again, know your aircraft well, don't ask too much of it or from yourself. Don't put you both in a position you might not be capable of getting out. Flying over high terrain when performance is an issue, is like, for a sailboat to navigate narrow, shallow channels with light wind. You don't want to be there unless you really know what you are doing. Last, but not least, there is the weather associated with high terrain. From mountain waves to convective – or orographic – weather, snow, rain, crazy winds. What mountains have of beauty; they have of risky. Usually you don't find clouds inside a mountain, but the opposite is quite common, keep that in mind. Learn it well ahead, take someone more experienced, and never forget: your margins are already very thin.

Crossing seas is no less challenging. If everything goes well, it goes well. But when it goes wrong, can go very wrong. Communications are an issue depending of how high and how far you are flying. And if an airliner can have some difficulty even with HFs, CPDLC or even SATCOM, imagine if you are in a small single engine piston trying to get to some remote beautiful island. It can get tricky amazingly fast. Don't forget your safety gear – and their weight. Pay extra attention to navigation and fuel consumption: the farthest you get from land, the more limited your options are. Be ready for the worst, always. It's sad, I know... the poetry of flight is seductive. But the real world is ready to surprise you in unpleasant ways. Weather is always a factor, wind is usually there also, so do your homework. Oceans are the birthplace of huge meteorological systems, so keep an eye on the big picture. If in the mountains the local weather was your main concern, while on the vastness of the blue marble, entire portions of the planet may influence directly on what you are going to face during your trip.

Connecting places and people, this humble effort to surpass geography, is the essence of aviation. Honor those who have fallen before you in this endeavor by doing it properly with the resources technology has given you. Getting a comprehensive weather briefing, file a flight plan or requesting a flight following even if you are not required to, getting weather updates along the route and always, always knowing where to divert if something goes wrong. Take your own step over the giants' shoulders.

- 7 –
EMERGENCY ONBOARD
Aviate, Navigate, Communicate

The emergency never advises when is going to be on board. Every crew that left for their last flight, didn't know at the beginning of the journey that, after thousands of uneventful departures along the years, that day at work would have a dramatically different outcome. Just like in life, an abrupt end may be waiting on the next corner. This not just serves as a reminder for us to get all we may from our experiences and treat everyone around us the best way we can, but also recall us to have an extra vigilance at all times. Mild failures may be easy to cope with, but shall not take our attention of what really matters. And if whole crews have fallen into that trap, single pilot operations require even more focus: aviate, navigate, communicate.

These three words are put in that sequence for a good reason.

You probably heard often about crashes in which the crew made no contact prior the accident. Well, that is because, although they were in the end overwhelmed by the failure or situation that led to the crash, they followed at least this precious rule in which communication is the lowest among the priorities. The first and most important: focus on flying the ship. If that fails, nothing else matters. And actually, even for normal events, the priority is always to be aware and ready to correct, if needed, the flight path, attitude and power setting of the aircraft so it doesn't fall into what is nowadays referred as "undesired aircraft state". Before it was known as having kind of fix values to be observed. But that could lead to some complacency. For example, one of the figures was more than 25 degrees of pitch up. So, if you are at, let's say, 10 degrees nose up, you are perfectly within limits and would not bother about being even close to an upset, right? Well, at Flight Level 400, you are probably falling as a brick at that attitude. That said, anytime the airplane is doing something it should not, you are considered in the way to an upset. The name used in light aircraft training is commonly "unusual attitude". So, whenever you get in that situation, expedite your way out of it. Fortunately, most of us will only see it in training - like most of other bad scenarios, of course, that's why they are not called "usual". But we always have to be ready - for this one, especially in dark nights and thick clouds.

Something else that has a lot to do with this first item: many crashes began with a small and isolated failure.

Then, somehow the crew got so focused on the issue that lost the situational awareness, ultimately crashing. A classic case was the L1011 that ended up in the Everglades while the whole flight deck crew was focused on a burned bulb. But that happens all the time in general aviation and even recent airline disasters - as the A330 over the Atlantic or the Boeing 737-8 MAX over the Java Sea - pretty much fell into the same mistake. So, a way of mitigating that really serious and common threat is: aviate. Delegate the trouble shooting and focus on flying - or the opposite, if you rather mind the subject. If you are a single crew, do your best to isolate the fault while handling the controls, instead of getting into a dangerous tunnel vision.

The second point of our three words code of conduct: navigate. Now that you kept your airplane safe in the air, it's time to decide where to take it. All counts, from how many engines you still have to NOTAMs applicable to your alternates. From special procedures over the ocean, to a more reasonable choice of the airline preference. The scope is vast, and has to be adapted to your operation, naturally. But what is common is: some emergencies will drive you to land on the first clear spot you find, if any. For other failures, you will have time to address the situation to the extent of turning it in nothing more than an inconvenience. But the ultimate goal is to get yourself safely on the ground, therefore a generous share of your post "aviate" attention is given to in what part of the world that ground will be.

And of course, last but not least... communicate. Once the two first items have been accomplished, "advise ATC of intentions" like says the chart. And is not just a matter of helping them to get everybody out of your way, but actually a way of getting them helping you out - and they are going to be pleased to do so. So, take advantage of that.

- 8 -
EMERGENCY AND ATC
Mayday or Pan Pan

Ok, let's clear this out once and forever. Now you are going to communicate your intentions. Some emergencies may not even require the use of those valuable resources, and a good coordination with ATC may be enough. And remember, not everybody will assume your fuel is critical or that your ill passenger needs immediate assistance unless you make a point about it. So, if your current way of talking to the air traffic controller is not giving you the results you need, upgrade the talk, declare an emergency using PAN PAN or MAYDAY.

But when to use each? Well, the definition of MAYDAY is "imminent danger and immediate assistance requested". This is as serious as it gets, and although you should not be reluctant to use it, of course means what it means: you are in deep trouble. Therefore, the ATC and all other authorities involved will do their best to help you, and yes, they will get the whole system ready for your arrival – or rescue, if that's the case. We are talking here of engine failures, fires, fumes, flight control problems, loss of cabin pressure, and things alike. Fuel starvation can enter the list, of course, notably because not every place understands "critical fuel" the same way. But remember, MAYDAY is that old talk of "with great power comes great responsibility". Use it wisely, and the aviation community will be there for you.

The PAN PAN, on the other hand, means urgency. You are not in imminent danger, but if you don't get on the ground soon, you may get in the danger eventually. It is already an important sign to ATC, so be ready to get good assistance from them also. It may include an electrical issue that will get you on the dark in the near future, or an engine bad indication – usually by oil or vibrations – or anything that can escalate to a serious threat in a short period of time.

Be ready to give ATC all the information they need, like the nature of the emergency, your intentions, present position, endurance, dangerous goods on board and so on. Have also a plan for what to ask for: they are very generous, but this will make everyone's lives easier, including yours. Depending on the emergency, you may not go beyond the "navigate" item discussed on the previous chapter, and may end up on the "best glide, look for a field" mode. And regularly reevaluate the situation, to make sure you are going the right way. Nevertheless, if you are going to talk to someone, make the best of it.

- 9 -
RESPECT YOUR LIMITS
Be optimistic, not naive

You may feel inclined to think everything is going to be ok, and that is not a bad thing altogether. If in trouble, the last a pilot in command needs is to feel hopeless – or to have a second in command feeling that way next to him, if in a multicrew environment. But one thing is fighting to the end with your best resources, something else is only hoping for the best and doing little to help yourself. So, understand how serious the situation is.

Eventually we are going to talk again about emergencies, but as the old saying goes, "a superior pilot uses its superior judgment to avoid situations that require his superior skills". This one is known to be Frank Borman's version, but the concept is universal in all variants and we talked about it before. So many good pilots have fallen pushing their limits too far, do not join them. If you don't feel comfortable, don't do it. It's not fear, is not incompetence. It is wisdom. May be the visibility, the winds, or icing conditions. Do not force yourself into something you might not be able to get out of. As pilots, we eventually find ourselves pushing limits even when we are very careful in advance, and that is how we get more and more experienced. But do not rush into that too early. The stakes are high, and no one can afford losing them.

When it comes to emergencies, it is no different. The startle effect may be overwhelming in the first seconds, even minutes. But after it has passed, is time to think pragmatically on your next actions – actually, the startle is your enemy: first a take a deep breath and then, fight it. Resilience is the name of the game, so, bounce back. And understand how serious the failure or situation is. If you operate a fly by wire airplane and lost already two of your three hydraulic systems, there is no time to fool around. Get your aircraft on the ground as soon as possible. Many don't know, but a fly by wire airplane without the hydraulics is like a conventional aircraft without cables. It may take you seconds or minutes, but you are going to die. So don't waste your time overthinking it. The same goes for uncontrollable fire or fumes. Many have fallen trying to find a more suitable place to land. Don't take it for granted. Get on the ground. Period.

- 10 -
CROSSWIND CONSIDERATIONS
Crab, sideslip, de-crab and more

Is there anything a pilot enjoys more than landing with crosswinds? Well, I might be speaking for myself, but this is one of those moments when wisdom and skills are used with a rather aesthetic outcome from anyone watching from outside. But just because it is funny or beautiful, it does not mean that is simple. Imagine yourself flying, and while you are preparing for an approach, you get a challenging windy condition ahead.

The good side of it is that you are going to be more focused on the safe outcome of that approach, so chances of you ruining your touchdown, for example, are greatly diminished. It is not uncommon to see basic mistakes being made on good weather with calm winds, since complacency tends to kick in and get us relaxed. But how do high winds affect our aircraft?

First of all, there are limitations we have to observe. Some are imposed by your airline policy, others by the insurance company policy, and besides those, for pilots who are fortunate enough to fly their own aircraft, it is always advisable for them to have their own already mentioned personal limits.

When it comes to the manufacturers, usually the word used is "demonstrated" crosswind component, and that is not exactly a limitation: anyone that had flown a Cessna 152 long enough knows it perfectly handles crosswinds well above twelve knots if properly dealt with. But having hard limits on your operations, either by your experience or by the operator that pays your bills, is something healthy. In the airlines we are talking about crosswinds up to forty knots, and although such conditions would keep most of the light GA airplanes on the ramp securely tied down, in major airports around the globe it is just another day in the office, probably followed by a beer and some goods stories shared far from home.

So, let's review the three main crosswind landing techniques. Crab, de-crab and sideslip.

Landing in crab means you are not directly correcting for the wind. Instead, you are flying wings level all the way to the ground, while your nose is pointing into the wind on the natural reaction the airplane has when affected by any sort of crosswind. Although it might be easier since all you need to do is to keep flying in the direction of the runway and its aiming point, without messing with the rudder while flying, this technique is not practical for all types of airplanes.

Conventional gear ones will not handle it all the way to the ground, but tricycle geared, including narrow body aircraft can usually do it on wet runways with ease, and even at dry ones on very high crosswinds if coupled with a sideslip. But the wide body jetliners are those that take more advantage of crabbing, because their robust boogie mounted main gears can stand some serious twist upon touchdown, tilting the whole machine back to the runway orientation almost by magic – inertia, I should say – especially with the modern fly by wire systems acting on the backstage. The de-crab method consists on turning the crab approach into a sideslip during the flare, so it is so quick and precise that leaves no room for funny inputs by the pilots, and works perfectly with pretty much any airplane, even more when ground clearance by the engines or wings might be a factor, already at small bank angles. But then, we have the pure sideslip - the method of excellence for airplanes from small taildraggers to narrow body jetliners, which crabbing into a dry runway would end up in the grass, or single engine pistons that, without this technique, would ruin their tires painfully while touching down in a decent crosswind.

The sideslip method has a beauty on its own. It might not be as plastic seen from outside as the crab, but it requires a decent amount of coordination on the flight controls by both human and machines – yes, automated landing systems use the sideslip, and this is the main reason why they have relatively low crosswind limits. The Boeing 787 for example can handle up to 25 knots crosswinds, down to the roll out, even on one engine only, when the computers are on the controls. How amazing is that? Yet humans can land on much more severe crosswinds, simply because we can add some crab into it and, of course, we have the capacity of reacting in a satisfactory level to quick changes the computer would probably find too puzzling. Having said that, know your machine, and apply the technique accordingly. So, as zero crab landings are perfect for not so strong crosswinds and smaller airplanes up to narrow body airliners, they can be a threat to bigger jets in high crosswinds components. Use the pure crab or the de-crab depending on the conditions and, of course, on your airplane and operator's manual guidelines.

- 11 -
PILOT INDUCED OSCILATIONS
Flight deck wind

You must be wondering what we are going to talk about. Well, we just addressed the high crosswinds in the previous chapter, and in no other conditions, the PIO show up as bright as in those. Don't feel bad: from F-22 Raptor test pilots to Boeing 737 captains, and including many flight school instructors and students, this is a bad habit several respectable people have.

In Portuguese we have a very sarcastic expression to define it: "vento de cabine", or, in a direct translation, "flight deck wind". Yes, you got it right: most of your corrections on the controls were not even necessary in the first place. And could even be only a response to some overcorrection you did just before. That is why it is technically classified as "PIO", "pilot induced oscillation". Most of the movements the airplane is doing are a direct result of the pilot's inputs.

And if those inputs are not needed for any practical reason, then they are nothing but the pilot fighting himself using the airplane as the battlefield. How silly it can get? Well, a bit more.

You see even highly experienced fly by wire aircraft pilots doing it here and there, and many of these airplane types are able to distinguish the pilot's inputs from the wind effect, thus correcting the later to make our life easier. So, if you start correcting something that three flight computers already did, well, then it gets really embarrassing.

Some people got the bad habit from the basic and even advanced training from instructors that used to do it and made it look like the right way. Others had this tendency naturally, increased by self-confidence, and were never properly addressed by anyone they've flown with. The fact is that this is an obviously wrong thing to do. As you make large and quick inputs in a small airplane, you are exposing the airframe to loads it might not have been designed for. And if you are flying a big jet, than the whole inertia involved in airplanes that can have the area of a city block, makes these quick opposite direction control inputs ineffective altogether – not to mention what your passengers are going to experience back seating such a ride.

Well, I know: the idea on any approach, but even more when the atmosphere is not helping, is to keep it stable. And in order to do that, you must correct any small deviation before it becomes too big – thus requiring an even bigger correction. But when is it too much, and how to recognize you are one of the bull riders?

So, if you have the chance to record yourself flying during a gusty approach, do it. Then analyze honestly your performance and come up with ways of improving it, if needed. If you can't place a GoPro on your operator's 250 million dollars airplane, that's also fine: on the next time you fly into a windy destination, pay attention to the way you are acting on the controls – or how your colleague is doing. Do it gently, small amplitude inputs, wait for the airplane to complete its reaction before you do your next move. Most of the adverse airplane displacement imposed by the wind is momentarily, and is not uncommon for you to end up where you were half a second before without doing anything - especially if you have a bunch of computers assisting you. Pilots transitioning from conventional controlled airplanes to fly by wire ones are common victims, since they don't have the feel yet for what the system is capable of filtering. For one thing is for sure: there is absolutely no need to deal with the stick and rudder like you were playing the drums. It does not look as cool as some people think.

- 12 -
ENERGY MANAGEMENT
The speed trick downhill

Since we are talking of flying techniques, let's take a quick look at a very common concern most of us have in every flight. You climb all the way up to your cruise level, then, minutes or hours later, you are going to start the descent into your destination. Now, depending on your kind of operation, airplane, airspace, either you are going to judge when and how to descend or; following strict company rules, limits and ATC instructions, you are going to work out your brain in order to be at the right place in space and time for a stabilized approach a couple dozen minutes later. And for ego or operational need, the most efficient way you do it, is also the cheapest. And the cheapest, is also the one where you are going to save more fuel for you or for your company but, on the other hand, is the one that is going to put you closer to the up limit of the approach. By this, I mean, chances are of you arriving "high and hot". So, is it worth the risk? Yes, it is. First because doing a smooth approach is nicer than doing a smooth touchdown. Why? Because, as we are going to see in one of the next chapters, a smooth touchdown has too much luck involved, while a smooth approach depends on true skill. Want me to prove my point? Alright: think of a very inexperienced pilot flying a new aircraft type. If he or she is smart, they are going to approach as low as they can, to buy them room for correcting the glide path along the way. If they are not smart, well, chances of them having to ask for extra miles because were left behind the plane are highly increased, and, let's be honest: chances of him or her doing it perfectly on the first attempt are really low. In the other hand, any pilot of any age or experience can do bad and good landings – which depends on a lot of subconscious responses and muscle memory, and not as much of thoughtfully thinking. Convincing you or not, the deal is: some airports even require you to do what is called "CDA", or continuous descent approach, something achieved by a low drag descent, therefore saving fuel, polluting less and, naturally, being less noisy to the neighborhood. Too many good things to ignore, right?

So, how much can we push before it turns "fast although high"? There is kinetic energy, potential energy and chemical energy for you to play with. But this is not the point of this book, so let's be practical. Well, once more, know your aircraft. Study to understand the relationship between its drag devices and your wings efficiency; how the weight affects it, that tailwind components can get you in trouble easily and do your best to anticipate what is on the controller's mind while vectoring you. If in doubt, ask how many track miles and do your math. For most of the planes, altitude in thousands of feet times three in miles is a good clue. Nevertheless, as new generation wings get more efficient, doing it by four may deliver you some more accurate results. If you are at ten thousand feet and forty miles out, you are certainly fine in any modern aircraft. But remember that you have a long way to go, and probably is not going to be a straight line. More than that, if you are coming for an instrument approach or joining midfield downwind at pattern altitude, you have to correct for that too. In the worst-case scenario, you will be too conservative and fly leveled for a while. And what if you were caught off guard and is too high? Well, as you know as a pilot, engine out, the only thing you can trade for speed is altitude, and vice versa.

But here is the not so obvious point: if you are high and put your nose down, now you are getting low fast but you are eating track miles like crazy, which means you might not be able to correct in time for a stabilized approach and landing. So, how to get the best of the two worlds? Slow down. Look for a very inefficient descent to get back to the ideal glide path. Configure early if you need, up to the point of extending the gear and getting full flaps if you think is that significant. With all that drag and on idle thrust, you are going to get reasonable descent rates while your track miles are running out slower. Prepare for a smooth transition to a normal rate and power setting toward the final phase of the approach and you will be just fine. If still it doesn't work, ask for those extra miles, there is no shame in it. And remember, you can always go around. A missed approach is going to be easily forgotten. An unstabilized one, not so much.

- 13-

APPROACHES
Flying by the numbers

After nailing your descent, the time has come to the approach. We are going to talk about visual and instrument ones here, and since is the philosophy behind that matters, we won't have to worry about how to do the briefing, read a chart or interpret the instruments. This book idea was never to over explain things that have much better sources to be consulted for that. Let's get straight to our point.

First of all, the concept of a stabilized approach is of utmost importance. We cannot stress this enough. You need to have a safety window to comply with. If your operator does not give you one, then come up with one for yourself. "This is my maximum rate; these are my maximum and minimum speeds". Anything out of that range for more than a couple seconds or if those limits are repeatedly busted, go missed and start your approach all over again. Besides, every safety window has an entrance, so you have room for fixing the descent to a point close enough to the runway. The airlines usually assume 1000 feet above field elevation for instrument approaches and 500 feet for visual approaches. These are good numbers, and if you want to give yourself an extra buffer, you may be configured for landing at 1500 for IFR, for example – so you still have 500ft to address anything that was not caught before. This is especially handy in fast airplanes. That said, avoid as much as you can – if you can, totally – any "combat" like approaches. Doing a base too short, high banks, a glide path too steep, seldom converts into any real advantage. Instead, it adds threats to your operation that didn't need to be there, and quite often are behind ugly accidents. The same goes for shallow descent angles. Coming in too low just increases the chance of hitting something you didn't expect to find on final, and both high or low energy approaches will make it harder for you to touchdown where you were supposed to and/or stop in the limits of the runway. Two reds, two whites – or any other normal reference in a less equipped runway. No rocket science should need to be done in the final minute of a flight.

And always remember: flying, unfortunately, is not a romantic sequence under the sunset with instrumental music. Instead, it is an activity full of well-established parameters that must be adhered to. There's a moment for configuration, there are a certain amount of RPMs, N1s, knots, feet, manifold pressures, and so on. Get to know the right way of operating your airplane in the most standardized manner you can. Let the guessing work for engineers and test pilots – who will not exactly guess either, but have come up with the right protocol for you to follow and fly safely within wide margins. Knowing the numbers will make your visual approach similar every time. Pitch and power never get old, they will be essential if you get an unreliable airspeed problem and are even going to protect you from most of the optic illusions we see on approaches here and there. Besides, doing that will save you many last-minute corrections maintaining that localizer and glideslope stable. Any excuse for not using them?

-14-
SMOOTH TOUCHDOWN
The real goal

Well, I confess: the title is a deceiver. Chances are the first time you picked up this book you came straight to this chapter. Gotcha! As any Boeing pilot knows for a while now, "a smooth touchdown is not the criterion for a safe landing". And, if the manual of the most experienced airplane maker in the industry says so, who am I to disagree? Besides, this book is intended to instill a safe mindset on your operation, in a subtle way, yes, but here and there we must express it clearly, and quoting Mr. Boeing is a fair way of doing it.

We emphasized the importance of a reasonable descent, a stable approach, and now we have got to the moment where your back seat drivers judge the most: the touchdown. Yes, it does not have to be smooth. The main thing here is to touch where you are supposed to touch: if you briefed "the numbers", "the keypad", common points for short field landings, do it. If it is an ordinary landing, then the whole touchdown zone becomes available. The aiming point is just that: an aiming point. It is not like you have to touchdown right there, but it is an excellent mark to keep in mind, especially on short runways. And once again, this is not negotiable: the center line. You must aim, touch and maintain your aircraft just there. No matter the size of your airplane, nor how wide the runway is. After all, the habit makes the monk. The sooner in your career you stop forgiving yourself on the small mistakes, the sooner you will be able to avoid the big ones. Being an aviator is in great part this pursuit of excellence.

It does not mean, though, that you should avoid the flare altogether. All pilots, of all levels of experience, are perfectly capable of smooth and hard landings. Yes, hard landings happen to everyone. In the other extreme, doing a smooth landing is quite easy: the difficulty is in doing it on purpose. So, let's cover both cases. The main reason for a hard landing is an unstable approach, which if you just read the previous chapter, you are probably not allowing to occur. Yet, some energy states and even terrain and wind, temperature, pressure and weight interactions may surprise you in the last seconds. Add to that, optical illusions and the stage is set. The best way to correct it? Power usually works well. Not pitch, power. But as far as you touch firmly and do not bounce, you are fine. If you do bounce, then go around. Do not try to save a condemned landing, you might turn it into a porpoise and ruin the day. The safest course of action is to stabilize your pitch, apply full/go around power, and as the aircraft responses accordingly, then you turn the rather quick maneuver into a normal missed approach. Resilience is the name of the game: take a deep breath, bring your heart rate to normal levels and try again.

Now let's talk about the smooth ones. Everyone's dream. Well, I don't feel I can teach you such a thing. Nevertheless, we came all this way together. Let's try to do something about it. First: attitude. Your airplane manual is certainly clear about a range of attitudes you should touchdown at. It doesn't have to be at 4.73 degrees to be perfect, but something between 4 and 6, for example, is fairly achievable. After that, energy, always energy. You must get rid of it as closer to the touchdown itself as possible. Do it too late, and you risk floating, bounce, land flat or any other not welcome variation. Do it too soon, and you might hit the tail or the tarmac in a dangerous way. Specific techniques apply to different models and types of airplanes, so it is pointless to go too deep here in those. But what I can suggest is: the smooth touchdown is of no priority whatsoever. I wouldn't trade any of my firm returns to earth for a bounced or deep landing. Safety, and only safety, is your real goal. All the rest, comes with time. If during the approach, you flew by numbers, for the flare and landing itself, is more like muscle memory, subconscious high-speed calculations and luck, a great amount of it. Don't be too hard on yourself if you were hard to the runway. Everyone has a bad day. And if I did not mention this before, the approach speed on a jetliner is typically 1.3 times the stall speed plus 5 knots. On a small light airplane, is a bit more than that – use the POH value – so you have more margin. That is why you get the power to idle on a jet two or three seconds before touchdown, while in a single engine Cessna, is more like throttle back over the threshold and holding the nose forever to bleed that speed and touching down smoothly. These too examples are not exhaustive, and differences in operations exist throughout the endless spectrum of class, types and kinds of airplanes. Previous experience is very welcome, but not always directly interchangeable. We just get good on what we do a lot, and many times. Do not assume things. Instead, get a more proficient pilot to walk you through a new model until you get, yourself, proficient too.

- 15 -
LOSS OF CONTROL INFLIGHT
The most wanted

Although not as common as other types of accidents, the LOC-I, or Loss of Control Inflight, is deadly as no other. Whereas other kinds of crashes are more common and involve fatalities too, the LOC-I is by far the big killer of our time. In a study by the International Air Transport Association (IATA) of over four hundred fatal accidents from a specific frame time in recent years, only 8% of the crashes were classified as LOC-Is, but they claimed 45% of the lives lost. Other studies for longer periods show similar data. No surprise all spotlights are over this subject in the last decade. And all this dedication, has brought light to some of the most common reasons why crews, from completely different backgrounds, equipment and environment, perished along their passengers, in this type of accident. Very often, it started with a distraction.

We are at the age of distraction. The world is in our hand: our smartphones can do all sorts of things, connect through all kind of ways, and eventually, they can be used even as... phones! So, think twice before picking your phone while flying. Instead, see the flight as an opportunity to disconnect, to look around, truly; to devote attention to the world, to the people and to the sights, sounds and signals around you. This exercise of moving your eyes from that tiny screen may reveal itself like a whiff of fresh air to you in ways you seldom grasp.

But, it turns out, the smartphone is far from being the only distraction in a flight deck. If years ago you would get in trouble while folding big and colorful charts, now is easy to lose your grip while turning knobs that control a colorful moving map panel. At least, these are essential for the safety of the flight. Same with EFBs, since the electronic flight bags are often on the side of your seat, and messing with them means you are not looking forward. For airlines, this problem is well known as "head down" flying, because inputs into the flight management computers usually denote bending towards the panel close to your knee. And this is a reason why we have at least two pilots in any big airliner, and at least one of them should be actually flying the machine while the other is feeding the hungry FMC. The examples go on and on, and just a fraction of self-criticism will allow you to find room for improvement on your own operation.

Yet, the distractions of the daily basis are usually well known and we, humans, with our greatest gift, the adaptation capability, can cope with most of them, most of the time. The real challenge are the failures. The delays, the weather issues. All them can, as small as they might look in the early stages, break our sequence and get us distracted big time. To the extent that we don't know if we are flying level anymore, among other aircraft states. And from there on, is easy to become part of the statistic, and not all of us are lucky enough to recover.

Therefore, if we found the threat, we can and must find a way to minimize it. Besides the essential unusual attitude training, the speed up of your scan flow and your confidence and understanding of what your instruments are telling you, the key is on task sharing.

Many, but many, of the LOC-Is started with small flaws that became the center of the crew attention and ultimately, overwhelmed them. So, if you are in a multi-crew environment, is tremendously important to share the tasks among the pilots. One must be fully involved with flying the plane. This shall not be overlooked, because every second matters. With appropriate crew coordination, any non-catastrophic failure can be worked toward a safe outcome. Training must be very vigilant on this in order to equip the pilots with this essential ability. If you are flying alone, then we get back to our "aviate, navigate, communicate" chapter even faster. And remember: just jump to "navigate", once the "aviate" is fully satisfied. An airplane can be lost, can be mute, but cannot be *unflown*. Do not rush: even a light twin flying with a dead foot will not fall of the sky like a brick: plan your approach, give yourself some room, and come for landing. The adherence to all these tools requires the quality that we will talk about on our next chapter.

– 16 –
OPERATIONAL DISCIPLINE
Do the right thing even when nobody is watching

It is something you should have brought from home, since your early years, from your parents. Although I perfectly understand that not all of us had the privilege of a comprehensive education, eventually, our own understanding of the world around us, makes the importance of discipline obvious. In addition, if it is necessary for the smooth processes of daily life, it is even more essential when it comes to flying. And there's no surprise in that: flying is a life-threatening activity. Don't you ever forget it. I will make myself a bit clearer.

Like every pilot, I had my scary moments whilst operating. One of them was on my first ever landing in a real Boeing 737-800 with passengers on board. I was, by many measures, fairly unexperienced. Of course, I have gone through the whole ground and many simulator sessions, had passed two levels of check rides on the type rating, and therefore was legal to receive dual instruction in line training. And yet, even with dozens of flight hours in the simulator, I felt overwhelmed by the responsibility. My previous over two hundred hours as pilot in command in other models of airplanes, many of them with someone else as a passenger, were not enough to make me concentrate on the task. It was a good weather afternoon at the Brazilian northeastern coast, under ten knots headwinds, all perfect. And yet, I did not know if I should look out, look in, and felt all the weight of the responsibility of killing a hundred and fifty people if I did some big mistake right over my shoulders. Of course, it was a highly controlled environment, and my instructor was close to the controls all the time, walking me through those final moments of the flight. The uneventful landing that happened right after is much more to his credit than to mine, and it would take another three months and a line check until I was finally released to fly as a first officer. For me, after some elaboration, the deal became clear: I could not think of my responsibility all the time. My actual approach should be to do whatever I had to do, technically. The safe outcome would be a result of that. As passengers became cold as kilograms, and the flying itself became numbers in a panel, the heart racing days were gone for good.

The thing is: you need operational discipline to keep your flying safe. As we discussed many chapters ago, you might have a standard to follow from your operator, or at least from the manufacturer of your airplane. Keep yourself inside those margins, inside the legal margins. Do not bend under the costumers, bosses or anyone else's pressure. And most important: do not bend to your own pressure. If you are not feeling comfortable to operate in a specific condition, don't. Respect yourself first. By doing that, you will be assuring safety. It is your duty to say "no" too. Besides, you have to be alive to look for another job. It doesn't matter if you were flying an airliner, crop dusting, a helicopter, flight instructing, or just back seating even. It applies to all kinds of aviation and all levels of paychecks.

And since even the regulations mention it – "being of good moral character" is one of the nicest requirements for someone to become an Air Transport Pilot as per FAR 61.153 - it is in the interest of this chapter to make the differences between mistakes and violations. They are not the same and should not be treated as if they were. However, we are in a "liability" world, so... they might be treated alike, as we saw some chapters ago. Either way: we are humans, we make mistakes. And that is how we learn, so, as soon as you don't do too many, fix them fast and don't repeat them, they are actually a good thing. But violations, those are unacceptable. Knowing a rule or procedure and breaking it deliberatively is a form of professional suicide – if not literally, sometimes. Nevertheless, you would be surprised with how many of the violations are born as good intentions. Every time you notice yourself thinking of a way to save time or money in your flight operation, have a second thought on it: is it legal? Clever? You heard this before, didn't you? Same principle here. If it is, it's perfectly ok. But if it falls within a gray area, or anything darker than that, stop and reconsider. How would you justify that given action if something went wrong? "Oh, but I just sneaked down 30 feet of the minima" or "we were only 50 pounds over the maximum take-off weight". There's no such a thing as being half-pregnant. Violations work just the same way. Don't be that guy.

-17-
HOT AND COLD WEATHER OPS
From the sandpit to the winter wonderland

This is another of those subjects that vary immensely between flight crew operation manuals, and all will begin with your careful look at the supplementary procedures chapter, adverse weather section. If you are forever operating in the desert, words like "shamal" on the news, or codes like "DU" in the METAR are not going to be anything new. But even those yellowish landscapes have a significant portion of winter, making always important to review those practices when the fresh wind is over. The same goes for the even more complicated procedures required of those who operate in the white. If you are flying local close to the Poles, you will be obviously as used to see ice as a tropical pilot is used to deviate from CBs, but even a short summer may take an important share of your proficiency away.

So, when it comes to cold, remember the altitude corrections, especially when below -10oC. The compressed atmosphere is going to take you too close to the ground too soon. "From hot to cold, look out below", remember? In the hot weather, is quite the opposite: remember that RNAVs are not ground based like an ILS, therefore, they are very temperature sensitive procedures. Even when within the chart limits, you will notice the steepness on a warm day. Be prepared to arrive high: there is no "undesired" state as long as you have briefed for it and act accordingly. When it comes to low visibility, guess what: a sandstorm will blind you as much as an icy fog, and them both require extra attention from the crew. Once again, as we talked many moons back, stay legal, just to start with. And then, if it is legal and wise, proceed. And your flight isn't over until you are at the immigration or the parking lot: remain vigilant during taxi; it is super easy to screw up that part, and this grows with the square of the number of taxiways in an airport, times the English proficiency of ATC, plus the number of supplementary procedures.

But, if there is an essential killer here, it is the performance of your airplane in such conditions. Let's start with hot: and I am not talking about Hold Over Time just yet. I mean summer, desert summer kind of weather. Well, nothing makes an aircraft... – let me write it again: almost nothing makes an aircraft more vulnerable then warm temperatures. The warmer the air, the less lift your wings are going to be able to produce. So, more speed required.

And to get more speed, you need more runway or more power. Or both. No surprise we have many 4000 meters plus runways in the Middle East, correct? And even if the runway length problem is solved, you still need more power... and exactly when you don't have it. For the higher temperature will give you less dense air, thus less power and... the engine will get too hot, too fast. Too many things going against you at the same time, right? Not to mention the high elevation airports that get sunny summers as well. Ok, I am not going to reinvent the wheel here, and although this chapter ended up more "line" oriented, any kind of operation is exposed to these weather patterns. Just check your performance calculations, manuals, trainings, procedures and... before I move on, remember your tire speed limitations. When the heat hits the fan, that surreal rotation speed may get you too close to it.

Now, snow time. Do you love it? Me too. But ice is a cold killer, as silly as the statement might sound. It adds up to your weight, it changes your wings profile, and even against performance logic, may easily steels your power. Do never overlook it. It is just there, waiting to make you become a statistic. The de-ice/anti-ice stuff is overly complex to be addressed properly here, but if you fly to Scandinavia and the locals are doing it, you definitely should get on the line to get a splash yourself. Remember the run-up drills, don't get too close to other airplane's exhaust – this is not the kind of hot air you should be looking for – and most importantly, do not assume things. Use technical tables, well versed people information, and take the safest course of action. Not the cheapest or the easiest: the safest. Be aware of ramp, taxiway and runway conditions, they can get bizarrely slippery even with optimistic RODEXes and SNOTAMs – and that's why we now have the GRF - and of course, check the HOT table we mentioned before. The correct one; you guys on the B787 and A350, don't assume things just because they used to work on the heavy metal you flew before. Actually, your plastic planes are more time restricted then you might have thought. All done? Enjoy the view, maybe you will be lucky enough to see some auroras tonight.

-18-
HUMAN RELATIONS
Ashes of the mean pilots

So, in the end, the only real killer to aviation will be the teletransportation. I am saying that in 2020, in the middle of the worst crisis that our beloved and sentimental industry has ever faced, but I've been recalling this every time some tech guy comes up with autonomous flight unrealistic forecasts. We are far from it. Believe me, I have flown enough hours in the most advanced airliner of our time to claim so. It will come, probably before the teletransportation thing. But not next week for sure. And, made by humans, aviation has all the goods and bads we bring with us into it.

I started in aviation many years ago, as a flight attendant. It took me over a million passengers until I did the transition to the flight deck. And sometimes even that precious amount of human experience needs to be brought in to make things work smoothly. Even more from the right seat. Aviation is over a century old – and now we can even sort of say it has survived two major pandemics - and yet, being second in command requires decent human relations skills. Not that being pilot in command is much easier – in fact, is frustrating how much one can't do despite its higher rank – but without hierarchy on your side, things are even more tricky. And that is when CRM shines the most. Learn it, understand it, use it. Like David Branco, a Brazilian test pilot and author remember us, crew resources management tools are to be used from day one. If you are an instructor in a flight school, give your student confidence to share his thoughts, no matter what is his or her level. The same goes with your whole team: your cabin crew, your mechanics, they are your eyes where your sight does not reach, leave the channel wide open. The only stupid questions are those not asked. Speaking of it, the "ask, suggest, direct, take over" stuff is powerful. If you are the PIC, encourage it. It might save you. If you are the SIC, use it. It is rarely required to go beyond the "ask" part in the normal daily operation, but its relevance must not be ignored.

Know your place in the crew, give your captain all the data he or she needs to make the best decision, respect the hierarchy, but get to know its limits. If things are getting weird, speak out. If that doesn't work, intervene. Your influence, no matter how junior you are, goes beyond the weight and balance of the airplane. When we read Ernest K. Gann we easily see how far or not we are from those days where captains were gods. Those days must be gone. We are all humans. And although we have many failures of various kinds, in aviation we must do what it takes to be flawless. We bet our lives on it. As a captain, you have your boss too, and if you are flying for an airline, very likely the airplane is not yours: when it is written "operator" somewhere, it is not to you they are referring to. Get to understand your role as the airline representative. Because we are living in a liability world, and a pilot must understand it to protect his life and career. The same goes for a student pilot who is on a first solo cross-country. Remember our chapter about operational discipline. The airplane is expensive, is not yours, and just because nobody is watching, it doesn't mean you should try anything funny. I have seen more than I would like when it comes to young people flying around thinking they are immortal. And, if you have your own airplane, first, congratulations: that's my ultimate goal. Secondly, be safe, be smart. And as any other human involved with aviation, use your emotional intelligence. You might not have a reckless copilot to groan about, or a chief purser or crew control department to drive you nuts. But if you are not feeling well, don't go flying. Preserve yourself and those you care for. Flying is a precious activity, a privilege Homo sapiens have probably dreamed of since the very beginning. It took us 200,000 years to learn how to do it – I was going to say "master", but it would be too presumptuous, considering our safety records.

Once, as I stepped in an FBO to pay the fuel, I saw that small ceramic pot with the "Ashes of mean pilots" inscription. That got me thinking. And for the many years, thousands of hours and hundreds of articles that came after, I realized I just wanted to make that pot lighter. Would you join me?

-19-
BEYOND THE IMPOSSIBLE TURN
The dilemma of Caparica

Not many years ago, a Cessna 152 was flying over Lisbon, Portugal, when faced an engine failure. Restricted by a visual corridor at 1000 feet to separate the GA traffic from the arrivals to the international airport, the small single piston had even less room to play with. The outcome was sad: the airplane landed safely on a beach and sustained little damage, but it was a crowded summer day at Caparica. An eight-year-old child and an old man got hit by the plane and had fatal injuries. Every time such things happen, we can't help but trying to understand why the pilot did not do this or that, although many others say it is unfair to judge from the comfort of a sofa. I don't see it as judging, at least not the kind of analysis my investigation trained mind seeks in those scenarios. It does not concern me who was, individually, the pilot involved. And not even so much what he or she did. What really keeps me awake is why they did what they did. Why has he decided to land in the crowded sand instead of the water? With a tail wind in that beach when he could have, for similar distance, landed at a nearby emptier beach and with a cross wind. For me, those are the questions that really matter, because they lead to improvements in training, procedures, regulations, infrastructure, that can, effectively, save lives. The "why" is the game changer. "What" is just a way to get there.

Just like the one in the Portuguese beach, flying is filled with dilemmas. One of the most interesting nowadays is the automation versus hand flying skills. No doubt the autopilot does a real nice work most of the time, but is it correct to discourage pilots of flying manually? Is it even safe? There is no easy answer to this or to any serious dilemma. And maybe, there is not even a correct answer. We should, all the times, ask the "whys" behind the decisions, the crashes, and more recently, a new wave is coming. We have been trying to make aviation safer by investigating the flights that ended bad. But now, our safety records are getting so impressive, that some started wondering if we were not trying to figure out marriages only looking at the divorces. What, for that matter, do we pilots do correctly thousands and thousands of flights, every day, that have put us in a so comfortable position of being the safest way of transportation? One iconic example was the invention of the checklist, during the B-17 development, in 1935. The amazing Flying Fortress crashed just after take-off, and the investigation discovered that a control lock was forgotten during the complex preflight of the bomber. Boeing, then, introduced this ingenious tool, that we use until today, in nearly anything that flies. Now, if we adhere to the operational discipline, the critical tasks we might forget during long flows are going to be covered by a checklist and fixed in time.

The war is far from over, though. The safety records in the airlines are outstanding, but in general aviation they are not so great. And experience is not the only spice on this soup. Even the learning curve shows that little experience is nearly as safe as a lot of it, and some portions of the middle hold a big "if". Those few hundred hours when you are over confident enough to push the limits, but not wise enough to recognize them, in a sort of Dunning-Kruger effect we are all exposed to at some level. And since aviation is so specific in its operations and equipment, that can happen to anyone logging something different along its path, no matter how many hours he or she has in total.

Two great killers in GA are inadvertent flight into IMC conditions and loss of an engine in a multi-engine aircraft. One is more a matter of operational discipline, but training can rise the odds a bit, and we talked enough about pushing proficiency and legal boundaries. The other one, is totally a matter of training: no multi-engine pilot should be prone to lose control of an airplane that lost an engine. But often we see guys that misunderstand the concepts of weight and balance, performance, directional control, certification requirements, and therefore have no idea of what to expect from their light twins. The result, sometimes tragic, are rushed approaches when there was plenty of performance available, or a failure to compensate for the thrust asymmetry that leads to a crash *per se*. Remember: you are not supposed to keep the ball on the center with wings level, this could easily lead you to lose control even at speeds way higher than the red line on your airspeed indicator. Same goes with certification: the five-degree maximum bank is for the manufacturer, not you. You can use more if needed, as long as you understand the extra drag that comes with it. And keep in mind that multi-engine airplanes lighter than 6000 pounds are not required to climb on one engine, but that is not a maximum take-weight limitation. Do the math to know what to expect if you have a bad day and plan accordingly. And always, always assume you may lose an engine on every take off. Don't let complacency kick in, when honestly you have no idea if the emergency is going to be onboard or not. And, just to mention the title of the chapter and get back the single engine airplanes, the almost mystic impossible turn. No matter how much we practice power off approaches, slow flights, S turns... nobody really knows when it is too soon or late to turn back. Even because conditions change from one take-off to another. But the manuals usually say quite clearly that large banks should be avoided if that happens, and priority should be given to maintain your best glide speed and look for a place to land in front of you. Try that turn by yourself at a high altitude and observe how much you lose on the turn, it is quite something. Now, keep that in mind: the nice results the much heavier and sophisticated Airbus A320 at the Hudson river, and even more the A321 at the corn field in Zukhovsky have got, show that the impossible turn may turn out to be, guess what, impossible.

-20-
AUTO-FLIGHT IDIOSYNCRASIES
Do not delegate your life to a computer

Computers are based in laws of physics. They are precise, fast, and cold minded. Having watched a Boeing 737-800 effortless flying an RNP-AR approach into runway 02R at Santos Dumont Airport, in Rio, from the front row many times, remind me of how arrogant they are. A true skill bar for decades, now the approach, between the terrain and an astonishing view, can be done by anyone trained enough to program an FMC – especially when visibility drops. The one eighty-degree turn, perfectly kept at 15 degrees bank, while the Sugar Loaf and Corcovado are left around, is the proof that they just don't care. If the airplane was to crash, they would not bother. They are computers, and look at us like cats would look, for that matter.

But don't be fooled. It takes five pilots to do an ILS category 3 Bravo approach: three electronic and two humans. And that is because they don't give a damn, and even more because, sorry, but they are not perfect. Same goes with the RNP-AR mentioned before: the human pilots must be there to intervene if the GPS signal is lost or an engine stop working. We are needed for a reason, and will be needed for decades to come.

The key is that the software is capable of wonderful things, but is not good in dynamic scenarios as we are. That's why we have levels of automation. If you have watched captain's Vanderburgh lecture, he explains it beautifully. If you haven't, search on the internet. But basically, we have low, medium and high levels of automation. As you might have noticed, in the airlines and more complex aircraft in general, we use the high level most of the time. In a long haul, nearly the whole time. It is the "LNAV/VNAV" stuff. The airplane is doing whatever was put into the FMC. But, as we get closer to our destination, we start getting vectors, different descent rate requirements, and things like that. That is when we revert to the medium level of automation: instead of programing the computers, we put data directly into it via the mode control panel. We "pilot the autopilot", so to speak. And then, when we have something that asks for a quick response, as a TCAS resolution or *windshear* encounter, we disconnect everything and fly it manually – not so much in an Airbus, but I won't get into this discussion, the example was only illustrative. And flying manually is so much simpler and reliable that almost all landings in the world are done that way, and exceptions seldom goes beyond visibility requirements. The autopilots are particularly good in what we are awful: flying leveled over a magenta line for fifteen hours. But even when exercising their true talent, they need to be watched. Relentlessly. You never know when they are going to fall into some degraded mode, do some funny stuff or not hold the speed properly. It is rare, but it's there. Don't cross your legs and start reading the newspaper like it couldn't happen. It can, and it does. And you are getting paid to fix it right away. Be ready to intervene, always. Maybe it will happen in cruise at four in the morning, maybe it will happen during the localizer intercept at a foggy night. You never know, be ready. And remember the glideslope weird behavior too. You have the false one above, a vehicle can trigger the true one to get crazy. Do not trust anything but your eyes.

And a final tip: I was fortunate to start my jet career in the seven three, an airplane old school enough so you disconnect the auto-throttle along with autopilot. So, controlling the energy of the plane with my hand is something I learned in the very beginning. But many pilots nowadays come from jets that have full authority over the thrust all the way, and even those who don't, now flying airplanes that do manage the throttles down to the runway – or very close to it, like the Airbus and its "retard" call – are losing the ability to manually manage the power. Be vigilant, do not just rest your hand over the levers. You are in control. Override it if you need to, command the go around power if you must. Do not wait for some system to do your job. Show the computers who is ruling the flight. Show your airline manager you are needed. If the computers do a mistake, or if you poorly program them, remember, they don't care. The fault will be yours anyway.

-21-
SHUTDOWN CHECKLIST
The graveyard of common sense

Sometimes I watch a movie, or read a book, and regret I wasn't smart enough to produce something that good. The subtitle of this last chapter I heard from another pilot friend, João Ridal, and the best I can do is giving him the credit for such a precise expression that illustrates what I want to say in this final chapter. The world is over regulated, that is a fact. We built a super complex technological society that had stolen much of our so called free will. Aviation is not different, and by enforcing here the importance of regulations, procedures, training, parameters of flight, we are contributing somehow to enhance that characteristic. Yet, we must fight to not fall into the trap of losing the capacity of being inventive, creative, especially when things go wrong. As aviators we are not allowed to think "out of the box", but we must, for sure, know the size of the box very precisely, to use every inch of it. Non-normal checklists are not indelible clauses. In fact, they are guidelines, only, and at some point, the manufacturer even admits it can't cover all possible scenarios. That is one of the reasons we still have pilots, and will have for many decades ahead.

Be fair, avoid the pot we mentioned a couple chapters ago. Go out there, leave your desk. You are not going to break the dishes if you don't wash them. So, if someone makes a mistake, don't be too hard on them. If it was you, don't be too hard either. We learn a lot by making mistakes, they make us safer pilots. Be flexible, listen to suggestions, ask for them honestly, seek for knowledge. Take the subjects given to you seriously. Everything we are exposed to, has a chance of getting in the back of our mind, and may turn into the difference between an emergency and an inconvenience in the future.

Understand that you don't know what you don't know. And by that, I mean you have no idea of what is missing in your preconceptions about any subject, and the one of this book is no different. We must be humble enough to recognize our ignorance, although is much harder to figure out the size of it. And that is why this book is how it is.

There is no way of teaching airmanship. This is something one builds from inside. Therefore, this book was never intended to scrutinize the details of operations, philosophies, crashes, or anything alike. It is just a collection of themes, approached lightly, chosen to raise your bar, leave you suspicious, more likely to recognize yourself in a scenario that may become critical. By doing so, it is intended as a stimulus for you to do something about it. In 2013, an A300 freighter crashed in Alabama, United States, mainly because of an undetected discontinuity on the route in the FMC. It is quite easy to see yourself making something like that, and every time I see one on my CDU, I remember them and get it fixed. So, this book is not an exhaustive source, by any means. It is a living thing, with room for improvements, and why not, a second volume led by the readers feedback. The runway is long, but if you decided to be a pilot, you passed the V1 already. Maybe you are just starting in aviation. Perhaps you have ten times more hours than me. No matter the size of your airplane or how many pages are filled in your logbook, we are all committed to fly. And as pilots, we must be committed to do it the best way we can. And by best, before anything else, I mean safe.

This is a hard career. Only those with a real passion thrive, especially when times are harsh. And even though, not all passionate aviators go far enough, because there are just so many things that can go wrong, that we don't control. If is there anything I learned about it through my own difficulties is that if you quit, you are already out of the game. To have a minimum chance, you've got to try. "We shall never surrender", like Churchill said in a totally different context, but that applies to this long-lasting war of making a living out of flying. And even when things may have lost their sense, if we are given the chance of getting back up there, it becomes crystal clear how much we love it. We don't really understand why, but we have no doubt about the need we feel inside.

In an emotional polluted business as ours, some people are going to try to take advantage of your passion. Don't let them. The career is yours, and just because you love flying, it doesn't mean you don't need to get fairly recompensated for doing it. You know how many sleepless nights you studied for a check ride, or an exam. You know how many sunrises you watched over the clouds after a redeye. This belongs to you; it was your effort and health that made that possible. And speaking of it, take care of your health. We already have awful sleeping and eating patterns just by being part of a 24/7 industry, so in your free time do the best to eat, exercise, sleep, and keep healthy. Even because your right to fly depends on it. Many great people have lost their wings for deceases they could not avoid. Do your best to avoid the ones you can.

And once again, resilience is the name of the game. Breath in, breath out. I don't know if it is an option. Honestly, I don't think so, because many I see leaving aviation are either trying to get back or live forever longing for the time they spent flying. And I tried to convince myself for decades that I could not be a pilot, that it was too much for me, too expensive, too hard, and only as I decided to follow my childhood dream I found complete happiness doing something. So, the hard the times can be, and they will be, keep the faith, the focus and the hard work. Aviation has cycles, comes like waves. But in the end, it always prevails: we may have smartphones and high-speed internet, but nothing else can connect the world physically as fast and safe as aviation. And no matter how acute a crisis may look; it will eventually end.

As C. W. Lemoine, an American author, who flew fighters and reinvented his career as a successful writer and airline pilot, says, "make them tell you 'no'". Don't quit before you even start. Don't neglect your wishes, do not deny yourself the chance. The world is going to do its best to stop you anyway. Chose the right side to fight by.

GLOSSARY
By order of appearance

PPL: Private Pilot License
ATP: Air Transport Pilot
GA: General Aviation
FAR: Federal Aviation Regulations
IFR: Instrument Flight Rules
ILS: Instrument Landing System
IMC: Instrument Meteorological Conditions
METAR: Meteorological Terminal Report
ATIS: Automatic Terminal Information Service
NOTAM: Notice To Airmen
ATC: Air Traffic Control
VFR: Visual Flight Rules
HF: High Frequency
CPDLC: Controller Pilot Datalink Communications
SATCOM: Satellite Communications
EFB: Electronic Flight Bag
FMC: Flight Management Computer
DU: Dust
CB: Cumulus Nimbus
RNAV: Area Navigation
RODEX: Regional OPMET Data EXchange
SNOWTAM: a NOTAM specific for cold weather operations
GRF: Global Reporting Format
HOT: Hold Over Time
CRM: Crew Resources Management
FBO: Fixed Based Operations
RNP-AR: Required Navigation Performance – Authorization Required
GPS: Global Positioning System
LNAV: Lateral Navigation
VNAV: Vertical Navigation
TCAS: Traffic Collision Avoidance System
CDU: Control Display Unit
V1: Take-off Decision Spee

SECURE CHECKLITS

Robert Goyer, writing for Flying Magazine years ago, has worked some math over it and concluded that the fatality rate per mile was something around twenty-four times higher in general aviation than in the airlines. Twenty-four times. This means you are twelve times more likely to die in a GA aircraft than in the car that took you to the airport. We must do something about it, and this book is part of that effort. And that is why it is both related to a student pilot or a seasoned long-haul captain. To bring them together, so they can share experiences and impressions.

Many great people have crossed my path along the last decades, from my first instructors as a flight attendant to my last captains as an ATP. I was trying to avoid saying some names to not be unfair to those that contributed decisively to who I am as a professional and to many things you are going to read on this book and will not be mentioned. Karina, being Takassu or Petrere, are worth of it just like Babak Yazdani, Karmell Ohlrogge, Thomas Wheeler, Vincent DaSilva, Nathan Horne, Luke Grout and Ricardo Soares. My own wife Veronica Barros, who I met flying, was a role model for many people, myself included, and my Boeing 737 and 787 instructors should all be named. Many first officers, some that today are captains, should also be remembered, as some second officers I flew for as safety pilot sometimes remember me as well. The list is immense, but Alexandre Arona, Clemente Junior, Fernando Marcato, Thiago Vizeu, Adriano Bortolin, Roberto

Giannotti, Juliana Torchetti Coppick – a longtime friend, airline and agricultural pilot who ended up giving the book a beautiful foreword - Igor Felipe, Danilo Andrade, Gabriela Duarte, Guilherme Gouvêa, Rafael Santos (both of them), Marcelo Taborda, Paula Petean, Isaías Cardoso, Patrícia Procópio, Jorge Reis, Reid Sutherland, Chris Livestead, Ronnel Moyano – talking to him over the Indian Ocean gave me the idea of the book, actually – are just some of the thousands of amazing professionals I flew with. The early colleagues in the flight school should all be named too, but I hope they feel represented if I name only Rodolfo Ladislau, Rodrigo Anderman, Jose Jimenez, Lucas Corcini, Fernando Sardinha, Marcello Rodrigues, Felipe Araujo, Paulo Ardengue and André Toledo. Speaking of flight schools, Brett Sipperley, Cris Ibañez and Eduardo Faraco have given me the opportunity to talk to their students more than once, what accounts for an important share of my understanding of the needs for this specific public. Many others have contributed, direct or indirectly, to the next chapters ideas. Antonio Lima, a dear friend that have been following a close path to mine for over fifteen years, was the first to read the original version and suggested way more than this chapter's name. João Balduíno, Bruno Fazio, with whom I often share concerns and plans, worth mentioning too for their direct contributions, and of course, professor David A. Esser, who looked through the book in depth to make it much better than it was before João Garcia presented us both: thank you two so much for believing and highly supporting the project as soon as you heard of it. Other great references to me in aviation that became friends gave also essential contribution, like Lito Sousa, in recent years, and Gianfranco "Panda" Betting, since I was a teenager dreaming about planes, both have direct influence on the style and achievements of the book, not skipping great authors I admire like Christiaan van Heijst, Eva Marseille, Les Abend and Sam Weigel, to keep the list short. By the way, when it comes to writing, all my editors in the last twenty years have added something to my way of doing it, but Gabriela Nascimento and Denis Bianchini, for publishing my previous airplanes related books, deserve a special place here, and yes, the beautiful cover made by Barry Ross, a name so many of us are very familiar with. Raul Marinho, whose blog published my first ever article on aviation, days before my first solo, and Alexandre Sales, Luis Ribeirinho and Renato Cobel, who published many of the over a hundred that came after, also deserve to be mentioned, as the likes of Frederico Fernandes, who gave me my first column overseas and of course, John Zimmerman, who published my firsts articles in America. In fact, in Air Facts, someone else must be remembered. Editor Pat Luebke, someone who assisted me through those first English written endeavors, and left us in 2019.

Being ridiculously unfair to those I forgot or chose not to mention to avoid some extra hundred pages, and kind of fair to those not so nice examples here and there that also contributed for me to become myself and not something else, I would like to remember what I heard from my great Commercial Pilot Multi-Engine instructor and flight school chief pilot, Stuart Sampath: I don't recall the exact words or if he was quoting someone else, but he said something like "My job will only be completed once all my students have retired". And, in a way, although I never had the chance of being a proper instructor and still have a long way to go before I get there, this was the idea of this book. To get you retired, after a long, beautiful and safe career.

Enderson Rafael was born in Florianópolis, Brazil, in 1980. He graduated in Advertising at the ESPM-Rio and worked as a copywriter for several years before joining aviation as a cabin crew, in 2005, for one of the main airlines in South America. In 2012, he decided to pursuit his childish dream and got his Private, Instrument and Commercial licenses in Florida, United States, and has been studying flight safety and writing about it for more than fifteen years, with investigation courses in Embry-Riddle and CENIPA. In 2015 he started flying for the airlines, and today he is an ATP based in the Middle East. He has three novels and two non-fictional books published, two of them related to aviation. This is his third.

You can find the author on the Instagram account @endersonrafael

Photo: Antonio Lima Cover: Barry Ross